The Chronic Liar
Buys a Canary

The Chronic Liar
Buys a Canary

Elizabeth Edwards

FEB 2004

CARNEGIE MELLON UNIVERSITY PRESS
PITTSBURGH 2004

ACKNOWLEDGMENTS

Grateful acknowledgment is made to the editors of the following publications in which these poems first appeared:

The Antioch Review: "Perspectives"
Artful Dodge: "Hammer" and "Nail"
Carolina Quarterly: "Walking Home Hungry after Church"
Cimarron Review: "Sleeplessness and the March of Civilization"
The Cream City Review: "Lunar Eclipse"
The Florida Review: "Lindow Man"
Ploughshares: "On the Train from Boston to DC in Dead Winter"
The Portsmouth Review: "Fever and a List of Snow Cancellations"
The Southern Review: "The Chronic Liar Buys a Canary"
Sycamore Review: "Mise en Scene"
Witness: "Sunset at Frick Park: The Dream of a Curveball"

"Sunset at Frick Park: The Dream of a Curveball" also appeared in *Sports in America*, Wayne State University Press, 1995.

Special thanks to the National Endowment for the Arts and the Maine Arts Commission for their generous assistance.

The publication of this book is supported by a grant from the Pennsylvania Council on the Arts.

Book design by Elvis Zukovic

Library of Congress Control Number 2003103707
ISBN 0-88748-409-3

10 9 8 7 6 5 4 3 2 1

CONTENTS

III

IV

For my mother, Anne

PART I

REWINDING DOROTHY

My daughter begs me to make her sing again.
   I walk Judy Garland backward on the screen;
      arms awkwardly splayed the way the blind see

with trust first, then fingers
   curling through hay and her dog's warm fur
      just before she sensed a rainbow above the gray stage.

Such artifice: the string that swings the lion's tail
   a zipper up his shaggy back, the twister—fans
      and spinning muslin. And when Buddy Ebson almost died

from aluminum dust, they replaced him
   with a man who knew my daughter's crying trick:
      weeping gets you what you want. By midnight, she's won

the horse that changes color, six times replayed.
   Pay no attention to the man behind the curtain—
      gaze into the flames where a hazy parallel life

reveals me sipping lemon ice before Ghiberti's golden doors
   with my art students. A lover cooks white quince for me
      in a basement flat, and every afternoon leaks

pink and saffron. But it wasn't the same horse.
   For each shot they trotted in a different dyed mare.
      And rewinding, I realize she never wanted home;

having dipped her feet in ruby blaze
   as dancing girls twined ribbon in her hair, she knew
      where she belonged. Ignore the seams—semblance

is all you need to spin what you're destined to lose
    back into being: a daughter just laid down to sleep
        reaching up for more kisses. Or blinking dry snow

from your lashes as you wake in paper poppies;
    everything ahead, emerald–shimmer so that
        there she is again, beginning.

ON THE TRAIN FROM BOSTON TO DC IN DEAD WINTER

We skim effortlessly over ice-clogged backwater bays;
past mounds of snow-covered trash
and weathered signs that say "Ed's Lobsters"
or "No Diving" and I am suddenly struck
by how little of everything there is.

A woman beside me practices Italian:
Has your sister lived in Rome long?
Please get me a policeman.
Her husband clips his fingernails down to the skin.

We pass gulls dipping their bills into frozen weeds
and an occasional dirty swan
shaking its wings in the marsh.
The rabbit tracks weaving between bushes and trees
seem deliberate, like secret messages
to something just beyond the sky.

It goes like this for miles.
A man throwing snowballs at a train trestle;
a young girl scaling a barbed fence—
her dream as delicate as a match
cupped gently against the wind.

And the graffiti-backed buildings;
the spray-painted letters ballooning
on brick where someone swore
they'd always love
someone else forever.

LOS ANGELES BLACKOUT

—During which authorities received reports from residents describing
a strange mist in the sky, better known as the Milky Way.

The vagrant stroked his sleeping dog:
    a beagle mix he fed saltines and ham
        and carried in a sling he'd rigged

from a ragged blue windbreaker. He watched
    crowds scrabble out the sides of buildings,
        leaving half-eaten steaks or incomplete emails

to the dark. The salesmen bummed cigarettes
    from the coffee kids, and the barflies gripped the necks
        of parking meters for balance as they scanned the heavens.

He saw his sky was bomb smoke
    or worse, to those who had forgotten the stars
        were more than shapes on baseball hats

or good work; were the inky patter in the tattered
    scout manual he'd memorized as a boy:
        declinating tables for finding north

or home—when lost: how to summon flame
    from sticks and friction. Before looting occurred to him,
        before the siren's hive-scream shirred the heat

and divvied the city, the vagrant found the four stars
    that meant Sagittarius was hunting overhead.
        As the traffic lights dangled their dead eyes

over the gridlocked motorists,
    (now unsure what rules applied)
        he cinched his sleeping dog, stepped into the street

and waved the first car through. Then another.
    Through his intersection, he guided everyone home.
        No one noticed his bare feet or knew about the hound heart

against his chest; pavement-worn paws twitching
    as her lids slid across her milky eyes: two oysters
        lolling in liquored cauls—or maybe

they were shrouded moons, for in them
    he saw the hazy spin of wheels sliding into cream-lit fields
        and headlights striking nocturnal eyes;

knew one muscled shove would snap the cage chains
    and he'd be dog-loose—his whipping blood-tipped tail
        a flare in the rabbit-blur of stars.

A FAMILY SCATTERS ASHES OVER THE PISCATAQUA RIVER MEMORIAL BRIDGE IN DECEMBER

Not the peaceful letting go
    they had envisioned with the snow
plows gearing down
    behind their backs or me
and Ray from accounting
    walking into town for chowder.

Ancient lift cables moaned
    like frozen guitar strings
while the bridge operator
    hulked in the dark
control box; his cigar tip glow
    like a greedy one-eyed rat
sniffing the frosty air
    for the unusual. Below,

the iced jade river rushed—
    much the way the Abenaki
must have known it,
    or the Civil War vets
searching the bridge's dedication plaque
    for some resemblance
between the muscled bronze soldiers
    and their own ravaged bodies.

When the family tipped
    the cardboard box over the railing,
the updraft blew the ashes
    into their faces; down
their collars, into the creases
    of their wool dress coats.

They had to hold their hands
    up against it. Ray said,
"Man that's rough,"
    meaning the kind of rough
when numbers don't add up,
    not the rough of determining
where a father ends
    and dirt begins. I hoped

the son would think the feat
    his dad's last practical joke,
or the wife, a tender refusal
    to let her go;
or the sister—a payback
    for some deep childhood betrayal.
They shook themselves off,
    tucked hair into hats
and climbed into a Chevy Tahoe
    they'd left idling.

All I knew, was that I had just
    spanned the space
between two states
    and walked through the bone dust
of a man who had probably
    loved border rivers;
had loved loitering down
    at the commercial pier
getting in the fishermen's way,
    just to see what the sea

had coughed up. And I knew,
    being in sales, the trick
the wind could play. Ray and I looked back
    as the bridge man shuffled
out of his box; his rat hands
    held high against the frigid sky
as he kicked the dusty slush
    over the side into silence.

THE CHRONIC LIAR BUYS A CANARY

I

The name on her brown uniform said *Jeanette*.
She placed the bird gently in his palm—
its sharp claws dug into his skin;
a ruby-sized heart fluttered.
She explained the canary's eating habits
while he concentrated on her gray eyes
and the yellow flurry of birds behind her head.
He told her about the mating behavior of Brazilian lizards;
how at night their cries sound exactly like babies.
Dipping her arm in a tank of African cichlids she laughed
as a swarm of tiny wet mouths nibbled her hand.
He told her, speaking of Africa, that if you wear orange
the elephants will lead you to their secret graveyard
and how he once ate lunch inside a giant ribcage.
From her face, he knew she believed him.

II

Stupid bird. His wife had not wanted the canary.
It flung itself against the wicker cage.
He could crush it so easily.
When it twittered and cocked its head at him,
he pinched its beak shut. *Jeanette.*
He whispered it aloud in the dark. *Jeanette.*
His heart leapt at the very sound of it.

HERNANDO COUNTY CHAIN GANG, CENTRAL FLORIDA

Only the young guys get to be rangers
so at 60, my father took the job.
Good pension, but no gun—
just a nightstick and a radio.

"The fellows aren't all bad," he says,
"but they're sharp 'cause they got nothing
but time to think up ways to rattle you:
siphon the gas out of their mowers,
plink gum wads at your back.
How they love to watch you lose control.
And rations: bologna or peanut butter—
just like a kid. And bad fruit:
puny apples, bruised bananas…"

And how one day
he brought one of those juicy, jumbo
navel oranges from home,
put it in one of their lunch bags
and waited in the prison bus
with his binoculars.

They sat down on the shady hill
and it was Cal who got it;
a wiry, quiet man doing time
for grand theft auto and assault
on a woman who'd tried to stop him.

My father read their lips. *Hey what!*
Where'd that come from? said one guy.
I don't know man, it was just in here!
Let me see that, said another, turning

the orange around gently. *Holy!*

Maybe my father had wanted a scuffle—
scarred fists punching at cheeks,
a wrestle in the wet grass clippings,
some jeering. Maybe he'd break it up
and take away their afternoon cigarettes.

But there was no fight;
no trying to steal it away,
just amazement that an orange
could be so huge—which the men sensed
was a trick as they cautiously looked around
for who might be responsible.

What'd you do to get that, Cal?
And what had he done
to get what he could only interpret
as a sign; someone finally
looking out for him.

The men watched him balance
the thick peels on his knee
and waited until he had popped
the last wedge in his mouth
before picking up their garbage spikes.
My father met them at the bus
and did the head count.

Ten men all present.
So nothing happened.
They still had a long hot highway stretch

to clear that afternoon. No one
was going anywhere. Maybe not
what my father had wanted
exactly, but what he got.

YARD SALE, 7 DENNETT ROAD: *A VISIT TO THE MENAGERIE*

—This book belongs to Josephine Currier, aged 8, Portsmouth, NH, 1849

Moving three plastic elves and a macramé angel
with light-up wings, I freed it from the Christmas bin

and turtle-held the book's cracked spine—a dime
would buy the palm-sized zoo. Inside

the marmoset faces were wrong—too human;
someone's vision of what monkeys might have been

once, waltzing in silk waistcoats. In the margin
sprawled a child's antique cursive flurry: *Turn to page 10*

and nudging the thumb-worn paper I found
a berry-black jackal stealing coins from a girl's pocket.

I want a kiss Josie look on 31 and though the grizzly's paws
were as wide as Chinese gongs, the baby

he dangled over the quicksand seemed at ease—
nothing in his life so far had suggested

wicked endings. *I want another one please
see 64* where hyenas chased schoolboys

through whipping grass as the sky above their minds
invented cobra bites and preacher-warnings

of punishments for selling secrets. For instance,
who gave the warthogs nautical maps on page 85:

their toothy grins delighted as the yellow moon
trailed her phases off the paper's edge. And who knew

the west wind could carry sweet coconut scent
so far that the timberwolf would leap an ocean

to lay milk-warm on the sand. I paid the woman
in the lawn chair; my dime clinking

inside the money belt she'd strapped across her lap
as if, freed of her belongings, she would blast off

over the ranch houses. High above the fat man
gliding back and forth on the rusty rowing machine,

his stubby hand fisting an autographed baseball.
Above the girl twisting faux pearls around her wrist,

as though the sun's brilliance could authenticate them.
The yard sale second chance says it's possible

that a boy wanted a kiss so much
he planted his desire in words,

knowing she would move from page
to page as he had asked, and find something

fantastic growing in her heart—a final *turn to 103*
to see the diamond-crowned lion shake

his golden mane atop a snow-encrusted crag;
the faint penciled promise

spidering out of his roaring jaws: *Josie,
someday you and me will always be together.*

THE GLASS ALLIGATOR

is what my daughter heard me say so when
the elevator lurched and Pittsburgh slipped
away, she grabbed me, screaming. Dredge cranes ripped
up ochre earth stories below where men

planned the new stadiums. They'd found iron
muskets and Lenape beads and chipped bisque
dolls. Buried while the mills rusted to crypts
and dark hands doused lit forges. Now woken

by blasts, this alligator's I-beam bones
stir with life in river swamp. My girl shakes.
His scales of emerald-crusted windowpanes

flash sun signals westward. Listen. Alone
inside the lizard's eye, the glass sky quakes;
we pitch—then rise into his twitching brain.

AT THE CRAWFORD COUNTY FAIR

I am become death, the destroyer of worlds.

—J. Robert Oppenheimer quoting Vishnu from the Gita,

at the first atomic test, New Mexico, July, 1945

We stroll through rooster screams
in the poultry barn and sidestep geese

who snip through cage at wayward skirt
and untied laces. The PA speakers list the lost:

one snakeskin purse; one boy—plaid shirt.
America descends each fall on this

abandoned airstrip field where, forty years ago
the barkers paid my teenaged dad

to carry giant teddy bears and con
the midway crowds into believing any man

could conquer physics by thinking
through the shifting rows of ducks; as if

it hadn't been the pistol, but his own finger
that shot lethal streams of water. Not much

has changed: the milk-plump 4-H girls
still shove their hips to stay their lambs'

powdered wool shoulders so the judge
can gauge the blade span. For a buck you can see

Jesus' pierced palms float in a dusty mason jar
or hold a shrunken Congo head or try to meet

your hands around a half-ton hybrid pumpkin.
The carnies at the funhouse maze lip-shift

their toothpicks and part the drapes
for lovers who must face themselves repeatedly

in mirror blaze before they trip their way
back out to stars and solitary space.

I hustle my daughter past shadowed figures
swapping cash behind the management trailers,

and keep an eye out for a man with too many prizes
and no girl. She spies the carousel's wind-ripped flags

and pulls me tripping over power wires to hand
the man her crushed ticket. He lifts her light

body up. Within the ring of parents
held centrifugally against the fence, I watch her roam

from bridled swan to horse to find the beast
she thinks might blink its lacquered eyes

and fly away. She picks the leaping tiger,
choosing dappled glades and distant rain

and lays her hand inside his varnished jaws,

amazed at his gentleness. When she leans

into the silver pole that skewers his back
and her bare legs, the paint-chipped saddle trappings

start their shake, with speed, the children disappear
in blur (those old pump tops unfolding tin petals)

until I see him, as I knew I would, hunched inside
the dizzying lights; his cigarette's red end poised

before his lips. His hand licked thick with axle grease
twists dials until the Wurlitzer blares *Morning*

Rose. My daughter is becoming spun joy.
Out beyond, the parked cars crouch

and shimmer in the dust and he must
fight to keep his balance squared

as fractalled lights cast diagrams
against his brylcreemed hair.

When he drops his ash to flattened grass,
the shorn sheep lift their onyx eyes

stall-high; his muddled thoughts hit scratch
and hum at music's end; the silence

of oblivion whirs gently there—a sound
too soft for anyone to notice it or turn it off.

PART II

ANGELFISH SONNET

Instead of Amazonian basin rain
your wasted body's nudged against the glass
by distilled water, pumped and pure. Bastions
of your diseased mind crash as tainted veins

leak life: a dying brother held sustained
by rubber valves and visions. Priests call last
rights. Nurses leach the heroin out—look fast,
how he swarms: but it's no rival gaining,

just yourself: refracted angel riven
in mirror. What sham world would dare to cast
resplendent backdrops as your flesh shivers

and scrapes gravel. Translucent bones. Forgive
me. I should have known your sea soul—too vast
and filigreed to winnow through such sieves.

CORA CHASING PIGEONS IN PRESCOTT PARK, SEPT. 13, 2001

She shoves my hand away
and sprints toward their gray
gathering. But I see everything
in Kodachrome: Uncle Bob

in Quan Loi smoking Kools
on sandbags with his buddies.
Gram said he was on vacation
and kept the photos
tucked in her robe pocket.

My daughter runs through puddles
to cut the pigeons off.
Honey, you can't catch wild birds.
I'm trying to save her
from failure. I'm watching

for messages in the flickering shadows
of maple leaves on sidewalk grit—
magician's hands, all flash

and sham so no one notices
what's being taken: a son
on vacation. She's backed

a lame pigeon against the chain fence.
The Marines patrol the river
just beyond her blonde
body. She might be underwater.

Kneeling in discarded silver
gum wrappers, her fingers

close gently around its purple neck.
She can't believe her luck.

The remaining flock explodes
in a ghostly rush of wings—
like chopper blades
blowing the veneer off the world.

DÍA DE LOS MUERTOS: DAWN AT SEAPOINT BEACH

At night, the stoned teenagers build sculptures
of rock and sea wash. The new one
was all white quartz stacked high and stuck

with ragged black cormorant feathers.
They had slicked it with tan seaweed
and studded mussel shells around the base;

face up, blue pearl swirling as the sun
climbed. At the top balanced
a small white skull—a child's Halloween mask

clattering on a wet stick. My dogs stalked it,
taking in the stream scent of strangers
and burned logs. It wasn't until my lemon setter,

the hunter, snuffed her nose frantically
in the sand, that I saw the ladybugs.
Thousands crushed in the wet beach—

out of place, as if something
had fooled them into alighting here.
Day of the Dead, I thought, remembering

Miguel's accounts of the evening
Mexican graveyards flickering in candle blaze
while familes ate bone-shaped meringues

waiting for their dead to find home.
What he remembered most was the waiting
as the bells shuddered all night

in stucco towers and how bitter the scent
of strewn marigolds when he knelt
to light copal incense for his daughter.

I imagined my ofrenda twined
with purple loosestrife and black
speckled stones for Suella, my grandmother

who wrote poems for the Saegertown paper
and wore red wigs to hide her cancer.
A piece of trap rope for Deborah,

not dead, merely lost. A crooked bit
of driftwood for Gideon, a spaniel I loved
with the shallow trust of a seven-year-old.

All resting upon a cragged slab of granite
for the terrible death that is coming.
My beacon to the dead, and the audacity

of art; of approximate coordinates
and armored satellites tumbling through space
laced with greetings in all our languages.

I cast my shadow like a temple
over thousands of brittle, cracked wings—
misdirected pilgrims—how the lost

attract more lost. All those messages
waiting above the world: dead bells—
nothing where it should be, no one to hear.

THE ART FORGER'S PENTIMENTI

For Eric Hebborn, a painter who forged "first drafts" of major artists, fooled many leading art critics, and was murdered in 1996 in a Rome alley.

(Pentimenti means to lightly sketch several possible scenes or figure poses on the same canvas before painting.)

The brazen youth stares resolute and proud
and made of math: line plus light creates cloned,
dark figures. In shadowy charcoal shrouds

of smoke, the forger first sketched the boy bowed
gazing at sand, then towards Rome. No, Corot's
brazen youth would stare resolute—proudly

flashing his eyes skyward at hidden crowds
of angels. What's Truth? Though Turin's cloth shows
a dark figure's shadow, the charcoal shroud

is microscoped; the carbon date endows
his face two thousand years—a faint ghost glows:
brazen. All youth stares resolute. Too proud,

critics won't admit the boy should have frowned
at the sky. Or slept. The forger's mind grows
dark, figuring shadows in charcoal. Shrouds

of canvas whiten the room; he narrows
shrewd eyes to mirror and resumes. And though
his brazen youth stares resolute and proud,
dark figures shadow him in charcoal shroud.

UNFINISHED CHAPTERS

The Six Swans

> There was a princess who sewed shirts
> so her brothers could turn back
> into humans. She finished all but one sleeve
> so the youngest brother had to live
> with a swan's wing. It was very delicate
> and he kept it folded.

The Grandmother

> Continents stretch beneath me as I place
> Grandmother on the blue-green shape that means
> Poland. I unstrap the oak furniture
> from my back and arrange it on the hillside.
> Through the smoke, her gnarled hands wave
> a photograph—the corners
> of my face curl in the flames.

The Ants

> He knew they were ants because of the slowness:
> one perched on each knuckle, the symmetry surprised him.
> "How is it that you stand us?" they asked
> in their tiny screaming voices.
> "I thought that maybe," he said,
> "God sent you." When they tried to escape,
> he twisted his arm. This gave them the illusion
> they were getting somewhere.

The Thief

> The apes have bound my wrists
> with willow limbs and are fishing
> around in my mouth
> with their thick fingers. I think
> they want their sapphire back.

The One-Eyed Horse

> One eye sees what two see
> only slower, so he caught the garden
> dragging its train of hedges
> toward the river and the children
> sketching chalk hopscotch squares
> in his blind spot, stones
> raring in their sweaty fists.

The Mistake

> I chased a wolf whose fur was woven grass.
> When I raised the gun, he turned
> into a mirror and I shot myself.
> The men have been tracking me all afternoon.

The Fight

> When my angels argue
> over who gets to star in my visions,
> they rip up each other's gowns
> with their teeth. I see the ragged angel
> with the swan's wing has won again.

SUNSET AT FRICK PARK: THE DREAM OF A CURVEBALL

Are you deaf? Right between the thumb
and middle finger, how many times do I have to tell you?
The boy stares again at his fingers;
rotates the ball, huge in his palm.
He will not cry. I want to take him by the hand
and tell him his father is a jerk;
show him the old home plate of Forbes Field
only a few miles away,
its gold plaque gathering dust;
explain about Roberto Clemente
and how greatness hurts. I could tell him
this is a kind of love he doesn't have to accept
while I fumble around for some better idea
to give him. But what do I know about effort?
I have neither children nor father,
and will confess that I too, love to watch work
in its purest form. If only we could sprawl on the grass
and trace the sun's collapse behind the steel mills,
I could tell him he is as beautiful as evening.
Goddammit you're not listening!
Now, don't release until you feel the slip.
And the dream tells me I must give this boy
back to the wrong ideas of the world,
back to this last light caressing their faces
for it is likely that they love each other
deeply and that there is nothing
I can do to stop it.

WALKING BACK TO YOUR PLACE AFTER THE ARGUMENT

I passed one man
I could have touched.
Stepping over him in the gutter
I thought about his loves;
imagined a woman whose picture
he kept in the capsule
of a hollow tooth.

There was a black dog in an alley
mouthing a rotten peach
and neon and laughter
and rich people
who knew they were being followed.
I had to watch out for loose grates.
I had to tell the prostitutes
I wasn't interested.

You said you would wait
exactly one half-hour.
On Congress Street,
the marquee lights flickered
so joyously, I almost lost myself.
But then the boy with the boombox
danced by and I caught
just enough reverberation
to know the song was an apology.

So I kept going, picking up stride
as I passed everyone who didn't know

what I knew: that if you want happiness,
you have to go after it.
You have to grab its scrawny neck
and drag it down.

LUNAR ECLIPSE

The blackened sun passed over the moon slowly,
like a child turning in the womb.
We went back into the house and made love
awkwardly in front of the bored dog;
both of us thinking about your wife
although I was thinking only of her dark hair
and the quick sketch of her face
I saw from a distance, once.

Later we ate cold chicken
and flipped through magazines
in silence. An essay on Bolivia
with photographs of women
cooking roots in dented pans
over a bonfire. Your slender hands
gleaming with fat from the meat
were almost as graceful.

But the sun never touched the moon
even fleetingly. The dog stretched out
in front of the fire only appeared
dead. On the floor,
with my head twisted toward the window,
you stroked my hair gently
believing me discontented.

But I was thinking of fire,
of the women's arms still warm with it;
their rounded stomachs wrapped in skirts
the color of scorched apples.

ON THE HOUSE

You bum a cigarette
from the ham-fisted guy
who's been eyeing the lonely woman
in the corner booth.
She smiles at him sometimes
and sometimes looks idly
out the sleet-smeared window.
The bartender dumps chips
into plastic baskets.
The hockey game's on;
Pittsburgh's winning.
The jukebox music is all
George Jones.
Fingering the bolt
on the underside of the bar,
you sip your Iron City draft
and wait for your change.
You're revved up,
you feel like talking.
Leaning over,
you ask the bartender
if the chips are free.
They're better than free,
he whispers, dropping quarters
into your open palm,
they're complimentary.

FEVER AND A LIST OF SNOW CANCELLATIONS

You wrap me in old sheets, as my mind jumps
like the inside of a radio. What I am
straining to hear is the sound
the man, now walking outside on the beach,
might make if he suddenly realized his life
were three-quarters over.
Tracing my finger across the frosted pane,
I draw sleep toward me, subtly
like the voices drifting in from the kitchen:

Dover Fishing Club cancelled

He has made the flies out of peacock:
Velvet Olive Finnock, Marion's Tiara.
They are jewelry to his daughter
who hooks them into the hair
and ears of her dolls.

I hear you running water.   *Thompson Dress Company closed*

A spider wraps its silk
around the chipped fingers
of a mannequin.
The dot on its back
is the shade of blue topaz
burning.

You bring me
a rattling teacup.

Tree House Day Care delayed

In their blurry minds, the babies pull
hemlock boughs around their faces
and feign sleep.

You prop my head, hold
a cup to my lips.

Rochester Runner's Club cancelled

He begins the second half of his novel
where Jennifer "aches
to be near the professor."
His sneakers in the dryer
thud like heartbeats.

The tapping of spoon
against bottle.

Concord High Blood Drive postponed

The gym is dotted white with nurses.
The sound of old steel cots
scraping across rippled court wood
dissipates into dusty corners.
The dread they felt earlier
is returning.

The birches are creaking in the storm
and you are watching me—you think I'm sleeping.
But in my dream, the storm has stilled
and the man on his morning walk
has found our frozen faces
tilted toward the sun; his day turned

into the kind of solid surprise
he loves. He rests beside us a moment
while fishermen line up to touch
our weathered hands for luck
before pushing off once more
into the black waves.

BUYING MAKEUP

She's half-scientist, half-pageant queen
behind the lipstick counter
in a phony labcoat. Her powdered cheeks
and whitened teeth paid for
by corporate scientists
who melt vats of colored wax
then meet in glass skyscrapers
to finger swatches until the names
come: Cocoa Lane,
Apple Suede, Papaya Crème,

so that this girl
can rub Apricot Smash
in the space between my thumb
and finger where she announces
the true color of my face
lives. Then staring hard
at my hand's crux then at my lips
with all her dumb brain
churning to imagine me

as beautiful as Venetian dusk
where men scatter violet sprays
from crumbling stone balconies.
Only she can see the purple gray
of starlings patterning inside my eyes.

It's what the scientists had foreseen
when they held their tinctures up
and watched the fluorescent glare
turn into moonlight; the ancient glow

above the mall parking lot
where my stained hands shift
and bleed beneath what seems to me,

not rows of lamps but newborn stars
who've journeyed to behold the gift
I've just been given—

how to transform the mundane
into the extraordinary. For this
began as Buying Makeup
but now I see my lips forgot
to tell my hands, *say Ginger Bisque,*
say Coral Blaze and Phantom Kisses, Copper Dust.

"UNIDENTIFIED BOY BY THE MONONGAHELA RIVER: CIRCA 1917"

I have found the photograph
in a book on Pittsburgh history
and I recognize him instantly.

Grandfather shifts the heavy pages
closer to the light,
his hands trembling
as he calculates years,
cross-references stories,
anything that will tell him why
he has never seen this. The boy

holds a stone and gazes
at a coal barge sliding by in the background
while a slim white hand
he says must belong to his mother
extends into the picture;
tired of small boys and work,
dizzy from churning water.

Unidentified boy,
you do not belong to this river
but to me
and to this silent man,
struggling to remember why
he is suddenly here.

But all we have
is the sound of Grandmother
rattling dishes in the kitchen,

this lamplight spilling over our bowed heads
and a little boy fingering a rock.

Maybe it is smooth and flat enough
for a good skip and the gray figures
on the barge are singing
low hymns to the river.
Maybe the white hand is reaching out to him.

The boy cocks his head to the sky,
hears something, shakes it off
and everything thunders out of his hands.

PART III

THE PROPMAN AND THE ANGEL

He slips the revolver into the ragged arm
    of the couch where the same woman dies
        every Saturday night in Act III.

The handmirror she cracks in her death grip
    casts back his face in fragments:
        one small eye, half a mouth, nothing

shrewd enough to save the marriage his wife
    calls hopeless. In this second-rate theater light
        it all seems fraudulent: the cellophaned windows,

the duct tape repairs in the vinyl wingback
    where the husband sits and whispers *Don't leave*
        but means something else. No one should believe

in transformation, yet tonight he knows when he shakes
    sheet metal, it will be thunder;
        that rapping the dented cymbal will mean more

than midnight: a husband realizing he has always
    been alone. Two hollow butcher bones knocked
        on a microphone is the shot that drops the lights

and the wife into darkness. When she rises
    through the crêpe de chine gates, her eyes gold-dusted
        with glitter hidden in her sleeve, we trust

this is exactly what she had expected of Heaven.
    Perhaps what we ask of the imagination
        is impossible—the desire to palm its mercurial slip

and hold, tight-fisted, the perfect illusion:
    pinhole stars, an electrical moon—lit blue
        for night, yellow and white for fear, plus smoke

for disappearing. And this husband merely inches away
    yet, we're meant to believe, worlds,
        searching the stage for the faded cross

of yellow paint that was supposed to show him
    where to cry. His heart stumbling, the Propman
        lowers the Angel's wings off-center,

so that she has to pitch forward
    to keep them on, leaning over the cotton clouds
        as if she had just dropped something priceless

miles beneath her; pretending to ignore
    the black velvet hands parting the curtains
        to still the quixotic confusion of her wings.

WALKING HOME HUNGRY AFTER CHURCH

One wafer and a thimble of grape juice
is sustenance only for the weak.
I need the slurp of cold pears
down my throat's length.
I need to grind cashews
into oil with my teeth
and moan contentedly like an infant.

I stumble along back roads
until I smell thick stews
poured into tureens so polished
and intricate my tongue
convulses in its own sauce.

I long for the salt and tang of lemon
dripping over buttered trout
or the bloody wine brown sauce
drizzled on lamb.

The spiced grasses of southern India
reach me over oceans
and ginger incense wraps its tendrils
about my hands so gracefully
I can barely speak.

I need the purple duck egg
to spread its fat into my mouth.
I need a Chinese chef

to pad my back with raw silk pillows.

If there will be olives and ham
in an afternoon field,
I'll go limp in your arms, lips parted.

JESUS IN THE GARDEN OF EARTHLY DELIGHTS

Near Nairobi, the jackals sense my presence
and scamper in circles whimpering.
The guide, sick with fever
sweats in a tent by the lake
sipping tainted water
from shallow cups of ostrich shell.

At a highway cafeteria in Lyon,
I eat buttered green beans
and wink to the dark-suited spies in the corner.
Once, there was a woman here so beautiful
I made an iris fall into her hands
from nowhere.

In the afternoon shadows of Seoul
my lover sprinkles sand in the streets.
But it is an old trick so I leave
goat tracks where I step and whistle
hot alley wind against her face.

Munich: I hold a toy poodle beneath my chin
to amuse the children.
Jordan: I fasten badges to my lapel
and haggle with the merchants.
Only Dansk can make me cry this sweetly:
the sun taking its delicate sip from the Rhine.

I have told my Brazilian men
to rely on instinct,
so they rip up their maps.
They need new boots desperately.
Their enemies have heard

I can make weapons
out of tamarin monkey bones
and have started to spread
the old fires in the foothills.

SELLING COMPUTERS OVER THE PHONE

I am who they imagine:
in a navy suit yelling at assistants
or in a tight red dress with my black hair unpinned;
my legs brown from a weekend on the Cape.
I talk if they want to talk. I rook the ones
who trust me. But I'm in cutoffs
and a Pitt t-shirt, working deals, keeping
my margins up, getting bawled out
for late shipments. *I'm so sorry*, I say,
but I'm trying not to laugh
because Mike is giving my phone
his best middle finger
and Marion is making kiss-up sounds
and I've already hit my volume bonus for August.

And I listen to how much they hate their bosses
or their boyfriends; how they just can't find
the time to start that novel
and about all their big dreams for the future.
And Mr. Stoltz from Cambridge Ore
tells me how his ex won't let him see his son
so that it's my turn to imagine
this man crouching in a Camry
watching the kid play basketball
in his mother's driveway.

But I've got six invoices to enter
before the warehouse shuts down
and tonight I've got tickets
to a kick-ass band
and just behind the kitchen window
there may be a woman

feeling terrified and trapped
with one hand ready on the phone
the moment she sees the car door open.

EMPIRE STATE BUILDING WITH FIRST HUSBAND

I noticed his sharp elbows
as we climbed and that his arms
seemed wet with new down and it
was when he gently clasped my
eyelids in his mouth that we
finally flew. What top floors
can do to the feet. But we
are all used to these slow lifts.
It's the only way we can
ever know a body, how
we understand endings, by
that same circling of our lives.

ARRANGED MARRIAGE, GEORGIA, 1838

She watched him from behind the curtain
as he turned his carriage toward the house;
his John Bull tipped against the sun
as the setters nipped the horses' heels;
their eyes the color of plums in twilight.

The mahogany desk was so heavy
one of the black men
broke his knee on the stair—a pop
like a beetle being stepped on.
He swallowed his scream
as sweat rivulets dried near his ears.

Later in the garden there were cakes
and sugared raisins and a wax doll
with chipped lips and human hair. *For you,*
as the horses pulled on each other's bridles
and snuffed into the men's hands.

Beneath the fountain
the cousins found a dead sparrow
which they passed back and forth:
its limp head no heavier than a wet rose.

She heard breathing and turned
to find him behind her.
She thought of clocks
in darkness; how his hands
looked like two curled moons.

And the low moan that carried past their faces
wasn't the wind—but the man in the shed
ladling salted water over his swollen skin.

Oh tiny star of pain between my eyes.
Oh sweet Polaris, now a sheriff's lantern
forced against my eyes, my secret
maps, my burnished, nameless path.

IT'S SORT OF LIKE THIS

Things are just about even here
except for now the leaves are rubbing
their bodies against each other
but not for warmth for
there isn't a sound I hate more than a lone
scratch he said and I believed him

so that driving through town I was quiet
and he said are you sad and I said
sort of and he said well I'm hungry run
and get me something and when I looked
at him he shouted hop to it

loudly so the people began staring at us
and when I opened my mouth
they turned their faces toward the river
and said look at all the fish Jimmy

aren't they something and they were
rolling on their sides gazing up at what
I first thought might have been me but was
in fact the shattered, mirrored sky.

LINDOW MAN

Ankles deep in freezing mud,
the scientists kiss each other
and draw out the slogged black pile
of a man who feels the toothless suck
of gravity as he rises. Bog water
spilling from his slit throat,
as hands steady his fetal body—
eternally murdered.

Because his face is mud, shapeless
they give him a new one:
wire muscles from socket to jaw;
roll clay lips and press them,
thick snails against his head

then stand him fixed on plaster legs,
walking inside the glass case.
The plaque: *What he might have looked like.*
His head cocked, marble eyes snapped open
to the fluorescent lights; to what passes

for a sun and the scientists at home
molding their faces into sleeping positions
while in the frozen basement coffer

the real man clutches his stone talisman
with the bits of hair woven through it;
remembering the men
who came down in the spring;
and his scream which never
broke the surface.

CLARITY

It's reflected in your daughter's eyes
when she tells her first lie
and released in the tiny spray
of water from a snapped bean.

It's seen in heavyset fathers kneeling
in lawns searching for pocket change
and felt when you catch your lover
in a hallway, touching someone else—

think of smashing your Buick
through a bank window—
can you imagine the spiderwebbed
windshield—such intricacies!

The frozen faces of the pretty tellers
and the officer reaching toward you
with his translucent white hands—
two dusted, silken moth wings.

How the scuffed leather chairs seem so grateful
finally to be on their backs with the wind
rustling between their legs
and the crisp hundred dollar bills
fluttering over the marble floor like old leaves.

SLEEPLESSNESS AND THE MARCH OF CIVILIZATION

I dreamed Abraham Lincoln was leaning over a balcony
burning photographs of himself
and calling the diplomats his flawless French brothers

while above the prairie the clouds formed
into the shapes of eagles and the Navajo
who used to live everywhere, politely clapped.

Along the treeline, the monks were trying to hide
but their red lipstick gave them away.
When the gatekeeper handcuffed them,
they lied about the knives in their shoes.

The Vikings arrived looking like the Spanish
but older and less foolish.
They returned to their ships, laughing at the bees
flying on tiny leashes tied to their fingers.

There were nativity children marching over the hill
except no one was singing.
The wise men hid sheep
beneath their robes and Mary was missing

and as I touched the hair
on the back of your sleeping neck
I heard a woman's voice whisper *Stop*

making those meaningless gestures
as if winter were approaching
and she had come a long way to warn me.

PART IV

LAURA, FIFTH GRADE

I

Maybe it was her willingness
to let the boys pencil-poke her arms
or her calm compliance
as they twisted half-licked suckers
in her pale hair, that made us ostracize her.

She lived in a rickety lakefront cabin
with no mother, just a father
who wore Turkish scarves
and always said, "Bye Fairy Princess"
which seemed ridiculous to us
as he kissed her plain forehead
through their old truck window.

I'd jump Chinese rope with the other girls,
chanting "Cannibal King,"
stealing glimpses at her alone on the swings,
with her arms wrapped intricately
around chain; the diminutive arc
of her motion suggesting invisibility.

In the girl's room one day,
I found her cradling a doll.
Someone had thrown it in the dirt
and broken its eye; one plastic peach lid
fixed at half-shutter. We surprised each other—
her pinched mouth whispered, "Oh"
as she stared down at her worn sandals

waiting for whatever it was I was going to do.

If she had said, "Get lost,"
or lunged out wildly,
I could have backed away,
obeying the instinct that urges us
to shun the weak; the same force
in the school nature film
where the eaglet pecked its sister
to death, one nest and no means to fly—

instead she said, "Look what they did,"
and so reaching out cautiously,
I helped tilt the doll gently under
the faucet; our six small white hands
bleeding mud into the porcelain.

II

From then on she'd smile at me,
her soft teeth sickly translucent
and making sure no one was watching,
I'd smile back—fascinated
that she took my little half-friendship
as if it were true; the kind
you prick your thumbs for.

I didn't know then, I'd get news
of her living in a shelter and details
of the marriage that had led her there;

that the little girl roaming in and out
of days, benumbed, had clung
to the chain of a swing
as if it were someone's arm
strong enough to hoist her into a world
where all girls are princesses
the way fathers see them;

where you're allowed to disregard
instinct's labyrinthine tangle
calling for hierarchy
to dig in and renew itself:
silt separating from stone,
shoots wrenching
their green selves from sedge

as gradually, the things of the world
start staking out original dominion
over this leaf, this meadow
as if it were nothing, perfunctory.

And you, with your pallid blue eyes—
a shaky punctuation
to a face seemed made of nothing
more than embryonic milk and memory
of how nature always wraps herself in splendor

before she stuns;
the way the web's elaborate pattern
fools the bee into believing

he's alighting on a simple rose;
the way I'm forgiving myself
now, without permission.

THE NAME OF THE GAME

This is about doing ninety on the Pennsylvania turnpike
the whole way home and no ticket.

This is about the feel of a couple crisp twenties in your jeans
and buying the next few rounds.

This is about telling the man who runs the hardware store
to "Hang in till Friday" while he nods and rings you up.
Not because you believe in Fridays
but because you want him to know
you understand the cyclical joy
of manual labor and long rest.

This is about the confidence of holding an unopened letter
you know says he loves you in it at least twice.

About the Pirates being up nine games over the Reds.

About how you can tell people at parties
that you find ballet boring
and prefer badly dubbed kung fu movies
where you understand the leaps better.

This is about doing a quick jazzy shuffle
in front of Kaufmann's department store
because it's sunny and no one's watching.

About the way the world sweeps you up on certain days
and lets you be a part of it.

I don't know about you,
but I'm doing much better

than you might imagine. Believe me,
this isn't about love or even happiness
for that matter, it's about winning.

MISE EN SCENE

It is late March and you still haven't called.
The fireplace spits its bright teeth at me.
The clouds are cowering like soldiers in the corner of the sky.
I have been measuring distances by the length of a cigarette.
I have been thinking of you and your old German films
where women pull giblets from their pockets
and scatter them to spoiled dogs.

If you hadn't left in broad daylight,
I might have kept a shred of sadness.
If this had anything to do with art,
I'd drape my body like lavender linen over the chairs
and laugh in black and white.
From an old yearbook, I would cut out faces
and arrange them in order by kindness.

How often I think of you
when I hear the scream of a child
who has burned her hand
on a bare light bulb. It is still
late March as the angles of the room
bend their black lines over me
like a calculated cage of spider legs.

MANIPULATORS OF LIGHT

On Bolt Run Road I almost killed a man;
my headlights pinned his body
against the pines, his eyes wild.
I screeched within feet before he ran off
leaving me shaking; an explosion in my chest

like the lightning bugs my father smeared
over our wrists and fingers at dusk.
We paraded around the backyard
flaunting our luminous jewelry
until the green glow faded.

It's what's captured in photographs—
the yellow sun streak that slashes
through a face or your brother's
red eyes, suddenly evil
on a summer picnic or consider

the night we spied on the minister
hunched over in the church basement,
working on his dangerous secret.
How his robes whipped around the flashlight
when he chased us into the cornfield.

We can take light anywhere now,
inside my grandmother's chest
where the doctor points out
the spreading clouds
of cancer on the x-ray

or infrared at midnight
exposing bats sipping

from soft cattle bellies;
their grinning, pinched faces
dappled with blood

and hiding behind the lens
photographers—dusky elves
clutching wires etched against the night
like ancient beings summoning fire.

At the first sign of trouble, they squeal
and beat branches then scamper off
to meet each other's hands
in the darkness and regroup.

PERSPECTIVES

While my uncle smoked pot
with his college students,
my brother and I were watching ants
crawl around rain puddles in the backyard
when one of the students came out,
knelt in the mud and began
to make the ant kingdom.

His hands gently folded leaves
into tiny boats; sticks and ferns
became bridges. He asked us
to find a strong piece of bark
for the dock and all day we gathered moss
and made houses and roads for the ants.

They needed a rock for the middle of the sea
where they could rest, so we scrambled
to find one flat on top. We stockpiled wild
blueberries for them and he held our fingers,
showing us how to braid blades
of grass to tie the boats.

I don't remember his name
but at dusk when the students inside
called him to go home, he stood up,
wiped his hands on his jeans
and left us kneeling in the puddle.

For days we placed the ants in their leaf boats
and nudged them gently across the water
until the rain washed it all away.

I know the guy was stoned.
I know the ants did not want us
to touch them. Still I continue
the construction. Notice how furiously
I build these tiny kingdoms; the kind
that don't last, the ones in which I live.

HAMMER

Widow maker, hambone, judge's lackey.
A promise hurled through the night sky.

You dream of boy's caresses in the garden
and star in the film where the man strikes gold

and loses his soul. In crowds you avert your eyes
and pray at the base of the maple. Even the cat

steps over you on her way to the robins
where you lay in the grass next to the dead

woman the police have been searching for.
In your neck's length you feel a man, miles away

wash off his hands to tuck the covers
under a daughter's chin. You find yourself

longing for your little hook in the basement
and the mice who looked to you for strength

as your round cold mouth longs to ring out
its only tone; beginning the old song

about how love needs fear
to keep its feeble heart alive.

NAIL

Rotten tooth, point of contention, witch's kiss,
sliver of shade for a mayfly.

Lodged in the throat of a rabid dog
needling your way down.

Petal-stripped, jagged hewn daisy
screaming with your comrades
to be freed from the stairs.

Waiting in the carpet
for the bare foot of a lover,
you are a steel-honed crocodile wish

or a Vietnamese girl
in a jungle clearing,
her bamboo *non la* tipped slightly

as she balances on one tiny foot,
motionless, mid-stride, and terrified
she's heard the sound of snapping twigs.

AFTER GRANDMOTHER'S FUNERAL

What I'd like is to drive off 80 and go up Eddie's Run
where the mountain laurel blankets everything
and find a bobcat that eats from my hands
and meet all the women who died
giving birth to me.

I'd tuck daisy sprays behind their ears
and listen to their stories about Texas.
We'd read each other's palms and compare
the different centuries, proud
to be back in our sleek bodies.

When they become sad recalling
the taste of strawberries
after a hot afternoon nap
or the softness of a mother's lap
covered in corn silk, I would understand.

And when the beautiful man walks into the clearing,
they know I will go with him
because they remember how sweet
it felt to be earth-bound,

scented arms swaying in the breeze,
the way the hemlock
strains her blowsy branches
for the accidental brush of a bright red wing.

PSYCH 101 HALLOWEEN FIELD TRIP, WESTERN
PSYCHIATRIC INSTITUTE OF PITTSBURGH

A busload of witches and ghosts
and uninspired Barry Glickman

howling at the girls
in his rubber wolfman mask

stuck through with a bloody
plastic knife. I was an ivory-faced geisha

in the silk kimono my grandfather
had brought back from the war.

Julie was Medusa;
her mother's chemo wig

tied with a dozen rubber copperheads
that lashed out realistically

when the bus hit potholes.
Professor Hirsch led us along

the asylum's gold-flecked terrazzo floors
that seemed meant for something more

palatial than insanity. It was Julie
who pulled me quickly down the hallway

lined with metal doors. We took turns
peeking through a chickenwired window

at an old man with matted hair.
When he spied us and rushed the door,

shouting at our faces, we ran back
to the lounge to help

the functioning patients
glue paper pumpkin heads

onto popsicle sticks. But
they had discovered Barry.

He stood stiffly as they encircled him;
hands clenched at his side

while they stroked his nylon hair
and tapped his rubber fangs

and tried to tug the knife
out of his temple.

Their blank stares
seemed to recognize some scene

from their past—the nuzzle
of a cousin's collie who'd loved them

or even something more ancient—
how Cerberus tried

with all his brute heads
to keep the living and the dead

separated. The posturing Barry
had mastered drinking ponies

behind the school incinerator
had not prepared him for this.

Finally, an intern gently led the patients
back to the craft table

where we eventually left them
clutching their pumpkin puppets

and happily munching the M&Ms
we had passed out. Boarding the bus,

Professor Hirsch winked at Julie and me
which told us he'd known we'd snuck away

but had let us go. The word *hallow*
means to sanctify—what Barry,

with his spare face
shoved in a grocery bag,

wouldn't have understood
but was beginning to feel

as his dull eyes scanned
the October blur of bare trees

through the dirty bus window.
Now and then there'd be a blaze

of sportscar, or a neon beer sign—
like a life preserver surfacing

before a drowning man. Like
the geisha's powdered face

flashing its radiant moon
in the madman's window;

her primal eyes glistening with the secret
he had long ago forgotten, but before

her crimson lips could whisper
through the glass, she turned

herself into some snakes and disappeared.

RECENT TITLES IN THE CARNEGIE MELLON POETRY SERIES

2000

Small Boat with Oars of Different Size, Thom Ward
Post Meridian, Mary Ruefle
Hierarchies of Rue, Roger Sauls
Constant Longing, Dennis Sampson
Mortal Education, Joyce Peseroff
How Things Are, James Richardson
Years Later, Gregory Djanikian
On the Waterbed They Sank to Their Own Levels, Sarah Rosenblatt
Blue Jesus, Jim Daniels

2001

The Deepest Part of the River, Mekeel McBride
The Origin of Green, T. Alan Broughton
Day Moon, Jon Anderson
Glacier Wine, Maura Stanton
Earthly, Michael McFee
Lovers in the Used World, Gillian Conoley
Sex Lives of the Poor and Obscure, David Schloss
Voyages in English, Dara Wier
Quarters, James Harms
Mastodon, 80% Complete, Jonathan Johnson
Ten Thousand Good Mornings, James Reiss
The World's Last Night, Margot Schilpp

2002

Astronaut, Brian Henry
Among the Musk-Ox People, Mary Ruefle
The Finger Bone, Kevin Prufer

Keeping Time, Suzanne Cleary
From the Book of Changes, Stephen Tapscott
What it Wasn't, Laura Kasischke
The Late World, Arthur Smith
Slow Risen Among the Smoke Trees, Elizabeth Kirschner

2003

Imitation of Life, Allison Joseph
A Place Made of Starlight, Peter Cooley
The Mastery Impulse, Ricardo Pau-Llosa
Except for One Obscene Brushstroke, Dzvinia Orlowsky
Taking Down the Angel, Jeff Friedman
Casino of the Sun, Jerry Williams
Trouble, Mary Baine Campbell
Lives of Water, John Hoppenthaler

2004

Freeways and Aqueducts, James Harms
Tristimania, Mary Ruefle
Prague Winter, Richard Katrovas
Venus Examines Her Breast, Maureen Seaton
Trains in Winter, Jay Meek
The Women Who Loved Elvis All Their Lives, Fleda Brown
The Chronic Liar Buys a Canary, Elizabeth Edwards
Various Orbits, Thom Ward